A *FIRST BOOK* OF THE
UNIVERSE

by
Margaret Crush

Piccolo
A Piper Book

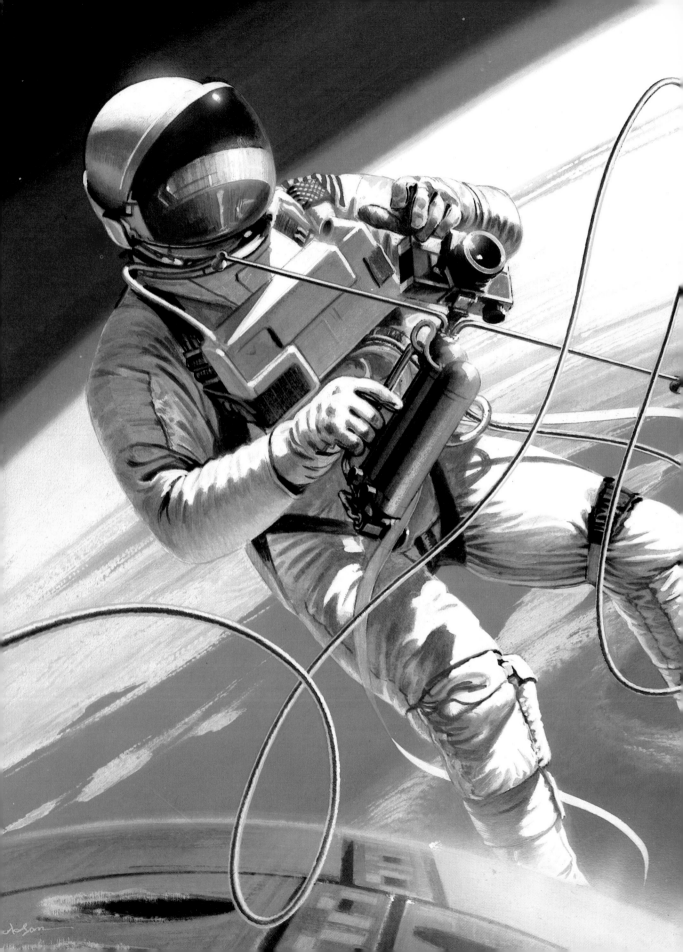

Contents

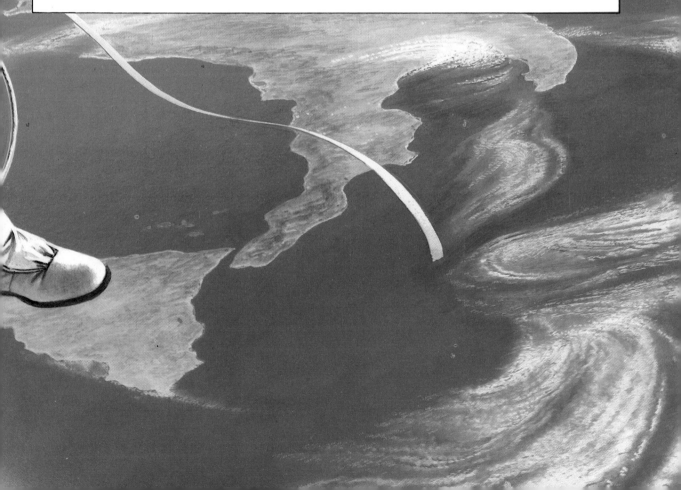

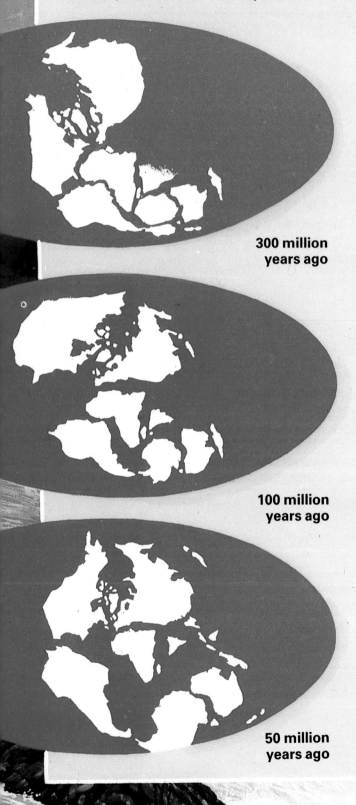

Below: How the Earth's continents have drifted apart over millions of years.

300 million years ago

100 million years ago

50 million years ago

A World of Fire

Millions of years ago – long before there were any people, animals or plants – the Earth was just a cloud of gas and dust whirling around the Sun. Slowly, the specks of dust in the cloud began to stick together until they formed a giant ball of hot gas.

The young Earth would have been a very unfriendly place. No life could have survived there. Its rocks were so hot that they were molten (or liquid). Fountains of steam billowed from the hot rocks and turned into clouds, which cooled into rain as they rose from the surface. As the rain poured back down onto the Earth, the heat caused the water to turn back into steam.

Then the Earth began to cool down. As it cooled, it became smaller and the rocks grew harder. They formed a hard skin around the Earth, known as the crust. However, molten rock sometimes burst through cracks in the crust, called volcanoes.

Rain began to fill up the hollows in the Earth's crust. The pools of water turned into lakes, and the lakes grew bigger and bigger, until two thirds of the Earth was covered by sea.

The Earth is made up of four layers. The first is the rocky outer crust, which is very thin compared to the other three. Beneath the crust is a 'mantle' of hot rock. This is almost liquid, rather like hot toffee, and moves about under the surface. The third layer, called the outer core, is made up of liquid metal. And right at the very centre of the Earth is the hot, metal inner core.

Although the Earth's crust seems firm and solid, it is actually moving all the time. Large chunks of crust called 'plates' float on top of the restless mantle. These plates, which carry the land masses that we call the continents, move about two centimetres a year. Over millions of years, the plates have pushed the continents far apart. And they are still moving today!

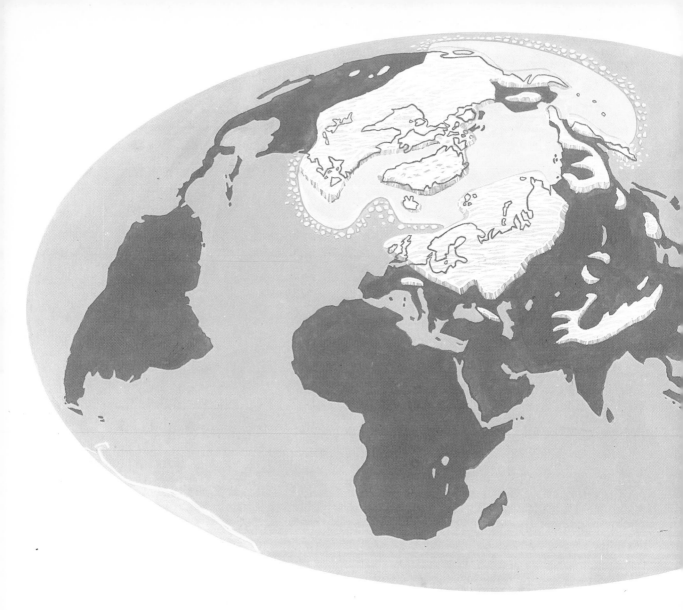

The Ice Age

Eventually the Earth began to look more like the planet we know today. Trees and plants covered its surface, and animals roamed the plains and forests.

Then the Earth began to cool again. Snow fell thickly in the long, hard winters, and summers became cooler and shorter.

As the weather became steadily colder, huge rivers of ice, called glaciers, ground their way across the land. Whole countries became covered by thick ice sheets.

Nothing could live on the ice itself, and at the edges of the glaciers only the hardiest animals survived. The first human beings kept warm by sheltering in caves and by making warm clothes from animal skins.

During the Ice Age, whole countries were covered by huge sheets of ice.

When the weather became warmer once again, the ice began to melt and the glaciers shrank back to the North and South Poles. These are the coldest places on Earth, and are always covered by ice. But the glaciers had changed the face of the Earth for ever. The creeping rivers of ice had carried soil, rocks and pebbles, which wore down the pointed mountain tops into gently rounded shapes. They cut deeply into the land, scraping out huge valleys like the one shown in the picture below. When the ice melted, rivers were left in the floors of the valleys.

Today, the icy North and South Poles give us some idea of what life was like in the Ice Age. In the frozen soil of Siberia in northern Russia, people have found the bodies of mammoths (huge elephants) packed in the ice. These animals have been frozen for thousands of years, and still look exactly as they did during the Ice Age.

The glaciers of the Ice Age would have covered the skyscrapers of New York.

Rivers of ice cut deep valleys like the one below.

The new island of Surtsey was formed when an underwater volcano erupted.

Ribbon lightning can be seen when a gust of wind blows the lightning sideways.

The Violent Earth

The Earth has calmed down since its violent beginnings. For most of the time, the surface is calm and solid. If it wasn't, we wouldn't be able to build houses and towns on top of it!

But every now and then, something happens that reminds us of the Earth's fiery power. Volcanoes still happen in those parts of the world where the Earth's rocky crust is weakest. When a volcano erupts, the mantle that boils away beneath the surface spurts through a crack in the ground in a fountain of fire. Red-hot rivers of liquid rock, called lava, flood over the surrounding countryside.

Volcanoes can give birth to islands as well as destroying them. The whole of Iceland, for example, was thrown up by a volcanic explosion. The world's newest island is called Surtsey. It appeared off the coast of Iceland in 1963, when a volcano erupted under the sea.

Where two plates of the Earth's crust meet, they sometimes grind against each other and make the ground shake. This is known as an earthquake. Sometimes the ground just trembles a little. But at other times an earthquake is so violent that great cracks open up and tall buildings topple to the ground.

Long ago, people thought that the rumble of thunder and flash of lightning meant that the gods were angry. Although we know

Ball lightning is very rare. But it is powerful enough to blast a hole through an aeroplane!

differently today, a big thunderstorm still sounds frightening, especially if you are out of doors.

Lightning can even kill people – especially if they are sheltering under a tree. It can split a tree in half, and crack a building in two. And its sparks can start fires.

Because that is what lightning is – a giant spark which leaps from one cloud to another, or to the ground. Its heat makes the air around it expand (get bigger). This happens so quickly that the air explodes, making the loud, crashing noise we know as thunder.

Thunder and lightning actually happen at the same time. But light travels much faster than sound, so if the storm is some way away, we see the lightning before we hear the thunder.

Hurricanes and Tornadoes

Wind is a moving current of air. The faster the air travels, the stronger the wind. Usually the wind does not blow harder than a strong breeze or gale. But sometimes it races along at around 300 kilometres per hour, destroying everything in its path.

A tornado, like the one in the picture, is a giant whirling windstorm. It is made when a twisting current of cool air sinks down from a cloud to the ground. Warmer air whirls up the tunnel at top speed, sucking up everything that gets in its way. Whole houses, people and animals can be carried some distance before being hurled back to the ground.

However, a tornado's path is very narrow. It can leave buildings just to one side of it completely untouched.

Hurricanes are tropical storms that build up in the moist warm air above the sea. They whirl along more slowly than a tornado, but cover a larger area. Their high winds are very dangerous, and they also carry torrents of rain. At sea, hurricanes can cause massive waves.

A hurricane seen from space. Winds spiral around the central 'eye' of the storm, which is always calm.

Tornadoes at sea suck up water, and are called waterspouts. The bottom of a waterspout is sea spray. The rest is made up of droplets from the air, like a cloud.

This is a copy of an old Japanese painting of a tsunami. The size of the wave compared with Mount Fuji makes it look terrifying.

The Power of the Sea

The sea can also be very violent. Big waves are whipped up by hurricanes, and can tower up to 25 metres. However, the most terrifying waves are caused by underwater earthquakes and volcanoes. These waves cross the sea as long low ripples, and ships may not even notice them. But as they approach the shallower waters near land, they rise up in a huge wall of water which crashes onto the coast.

The picture shows a giant wave breaking on a tropical beach. As the wave thunders ashore it will sweep along everything in its path, overturning boats and drowning people and animals.

These giant waves are called 'tsunami', after the Japanese word for storm wave. Many tsunami swell up around Japan and other parts of the Pacific Ocean. This area is called the 'ring of fire', because it has many earthquakes and volcanoes.

A huge volcanic explosion in Indonesia in 1883 set off one of the world's most terrible tsunami. It crashed over several islands and drowned nearly 40,000 people. It was not surprising that the wave was so big. The explosion blew away nearly all of the island of Krakatoa, and the noise woke up people sleeping in Australia, thousands of kilometres away.

Shallow continental shelf

Mountains

Abyss

Trench

Undersea World

Nearly three quarters of the Earth's surface is covered by the sea. There are four main oceans, the largest being the Pacific. This is followed in size by the Atlantic, the Indian and the Arctic Oceans. Most of the Arctic Ocean lies under the sheets of ice that surround the North Pole. Around the South Pole, the southern edges of the Pacific, Atlantic and Indian Oceans are known as the Antarctic Ocean.

The seabed, like the land, has long chains of rocky mountains, wide plains and deep valleys. Occasionally, high mountain peaks rise up above the surface of the water to form islands.

Around the coast, the sea floor gradually slopes away from the land. It then flattens out to form a plain, which we call the continental shelf. In places, the shelf stretches out for hundreds of kilometres into the sea. Most of the plants and fish in the sea are found in these waters, where there is plenty of light and warmth from the Sun.

Along the edges of the shelf, the ocean floor plunges down steeply to a very great depth. This part of the ocean floor is called the abyss. It is split in places by even deeper trenches.

Deepest of all is the Marianas Trench in the Pacific Ocean. If you took Mount Everest, the tallest mountain in the world, and put it in the Marianas Trench, the walls of the trench would rise high above the mountain peak.

Although the sea forms such a big part of the Earth, we know very little about it. People wearing snorkels and flippers can swim around in shallow waters. Submarines and deep-sea divers carrying air supplies can explore still further. But in very deep places, the weight of the water would crush an ordinary submarine. However, special underwater craft called bathyscaphes have been made which are strong enough to stand the pressure of the water. The bathyscaphe *Trieste* in the picture has even explored the Marianas Trench, probing the inky blackness with its powerful lights.

To explore the undersea world properly, scientists need underwater laboratories where they can live and work for several weeks.

Sealab III is a laboratory which rests on the seabed. It is rather like an underwater 'space station', and has a crew of divers called 'aquanauts'.

POST.

Mercury Venus Earth Mars

Sun

The Earth in Space

Our Earth is one of nine planets which circle a star called the Sun. The Sun and its planets are called the 'solar system'. Mercury is the nearest to the Sun, followed by Venus, Earth, Mars, Jupiter, Saturn, Uranus, Neptune and Pluto.

When the Sun was forming, it threw off whirling rings of gas and dust.

Each of the planets moves around the Sun in a circular path called an 'orbit'. The nearer the planet is to the Sun, the less time it takes to make a complete orbit. On Earth, one orbit takes about 365¼ days, and is called a year. Mercury takes 88 Earth days, but faraway Pluto takes 248 Earth years. The planets also spin as they travel around the Sun. The Earth takes 24 hours to spin once, which gives us one day. It is orbited by a small rocky body called the Moon. Mars, Jupiter, Saturn, Uranus and Neptune all have moons, too.

Planets do not give out light of their own, but stars like the Sun burn brightly. The planets of our solar system get all their light from the Sun and only appear to shine because they reflect the Sun's light.

Gradually, the gas and dust formed into solid planets orbiting the Sun.

The Moon

The ancient Romans believed that the Moon was a silver chariot driven by the goddess Diana across the sky every night. Other people thought it was made of cheese. And for hundreds of years, people dreamed of visiting the Moon.

But until recently, this seemed impossible. No engine was fast enough to break away from the Earth's gravity. Gravity is the 'pulling' force made by a star or planet as it spins around in space. This 'pull' means that smaller objects are attracted to it like a magnet.

The journey to the Moon was made possible by the development of the rocket. Rockets are like huge, powerful fireworks that give spacecraft enough speed to escape the Earth's gravity altogether.

The first spacecraft to explore the Moon were unmanned 'probes' that were controlled from Earth. Probes sent back the first close-up photographs of the Moon's surface. Some, like *Surveyor III* shown here (**1**), made landings on the Moon to find out whether it was safe for people to follow.

In 1969, the United States sent three astronauts to the Moon. The first man on the surface was Neil

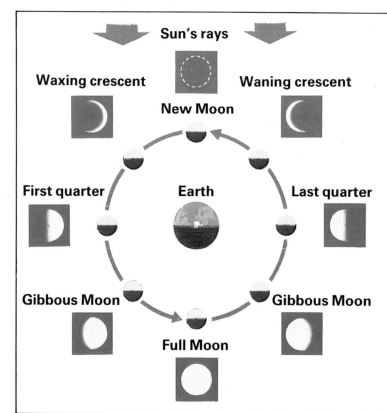

Sun's rays

Waxing crescent

New Moon

Waning crescent

First quarter

Earth

Last quarter

Gibbous Moon

Full Moon

Gibbous Moon

The Earth's gravity keeps the Moon in orbit around it.

The Moon appears to shine because it reflects light from the Sun. When the Moon is between the Earth and the Sun, its lit-up side is turned away from us, and it is invisible (a new Moon). But as it moves round the Earth, we see more of its lit-up surface. At first we see a thin crescent, then a half Moon (called the 'First Quarter'), and then a gibbous Moon. Finally, when the Moon is opposite the Sun in the sky, we see it as the full Moon. As the Moon moves from new to full, it is said to be 'waxing' (growing bigger). And as it moves back to a new Moon, it is said to be 'waning' (getting smaller).

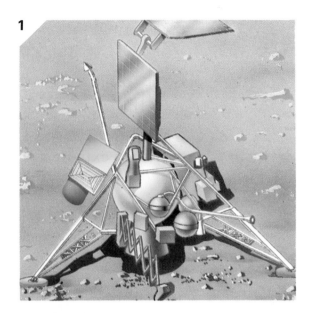

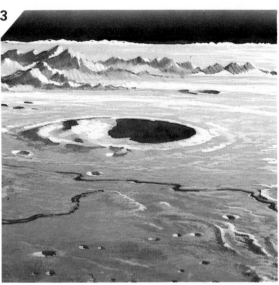

Armstrong (**2**). Although the Moon is our nearest neighbour in space, it is still an incredible journey – further than travelling nine times around the Earth.

Five more teams of astronauts visited the Moon, bringing back samples of rock and soil. They found that the Moon had a very rough surface with many enormous holes called craters, like the one shown above (**3**). There are also dark lowland areas known as 'seas' – although there is no water on the Moon. The 'seas' are probably craters which were flooded with lava. You can see them even without a telescope – they make up the shape of a face, which people call 'the Man in the Moon'!

A Furnace World

The small planet Mercury is the closest to the Sun. The side facing the Sun reaches an incredible temperature of over 400°C – hot enough to melt tin or lead. But it also has a dark side which is turned away from the Sun, where it is always well below freezing point.

Mercury is difficult to see from Earth, although at certain times we can just see it as a small black dot against the Sun. Scientists knew very little about Mercury, until the space probe *Mariner 10* flew past the planet and sent back photographs of its surface. Then they discovered that the tiny planet has many craters and lava plains, and that its mountains are steep and jagged. Mercury has no air, rain or water, and no life could ever survive there.

The Morning Star

You can often see Venus at sunset and sunrise. It is sometimes called the 'evening star' or the 'morning star'.

Venus orbits the Sun every 225 days. It is about the same size as the Earth, and people used to think that there might be life beneath the clouds that hide its surface.

However, probes have since shown that no life can exist on Venus. Violent storms rage beneath the swirling clouds, where the atmosphere is made up mainly of carbon dioxide. The 'atmosphere' of a planet is the invisible blanket of gases which surrounds it. On Earth, the atmosphere is made up of air, which we need in order to breathe. But on Venus, the atmosphere is not

Venus is brighter than any other planet. This is because of its thick white clouds, which reflect a lot of light back from the Sun. We now know that the clouds are not made of rain, like those on Earth, but of a strong acid.

only poisonous, but so heavy that it would crush a human being. It traps the Sun's heat like a greenhouse, making the surface extremely hot.

The Red Planet

When people talked of life on other planets in the solar system, Mars always seemed the most likely possibility. Like Earth, it has ice caps at both poles, and it has seasons of summer and winter. In summer, astronomers could see a greenish colour on the surface. They thought this might mean that there were plants growing there.

Some people even thought they could see canals on Mars, and wondered if there was a race of Martians.

But space probes failed to find any signs of life. They found no canals, plants or Martians.

Mars has two moons, and it orbits the Sun every 687 days. It is a rocky desert covered in large areas by rusty soil. Fierce storms blow red dust across the planet, making pink skies and purple sunsets. The cold nights bring icy clouds, and freezing fog fills the craters which cover its surface.

Mars is covered by craters. Some may have been formed by rocks crashing to its surface from space. Others, like the gigantic Mount Olympus shown below, are made by volcanoes.

The huge Martian rift valley Coprates was made by a crack in the Martian crust. It is 120 kilometres wide and 6 kilometres deep – much bigger than anything of its kind on Earth.

The Outer Planets

Beyond Mars are the four giant 'outer planets', made mostly of gas and rock.

First comes Jupiter (shown above), which orbits the Sun every 11.9 years. It is 11 times bigger than the Earth, and weighs more than twice as much as all the Sun's other planets put together. It is lashed by violent storms, with flashes of lightning thousands of kilometres long. Telescopes show a large red spot, big enough to swallow three Earths, which is made by a spinning whirlwind of clouds.

Jupiter spins very fast in space. It is surrounded by a swirling mass of colourful clouds, and these are pulled into bands by its rapid spinning motion.

There are at least 16 moons in orbit around Jupiter. Two of these moons, Ganymede and Callisto, are larger than Mercury.

Saturn is the second biggest planet, and although it is twice as far from the Sun as Jupiter, it can still be seen through a telescope. It orbits the Sun every 29.5 years, and has at least 23 moons.

Saturn is the most beautiful planet in the solar system, because of the bright rings that surround it. The rings are made up of thousands of tiny moonlets, covered in ice.

Until 1781, astronomers thought that Saturn was the most distant planet in the solar system. Then Uranus was discovered, followed by Neptune in 1845.

Uranus is a cold ball of green-coloured gas, which orbits the Sun every 84 years. Because its axis is tilted to one side, it has strange seasons – 42 years of summer followed by 42 years of winter. Neptune looks very much like Uranus and orbits the Sun every 165 years. Both planets have their own moons.

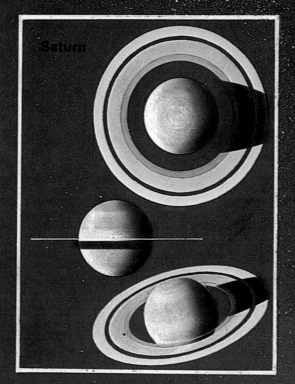

Saturn

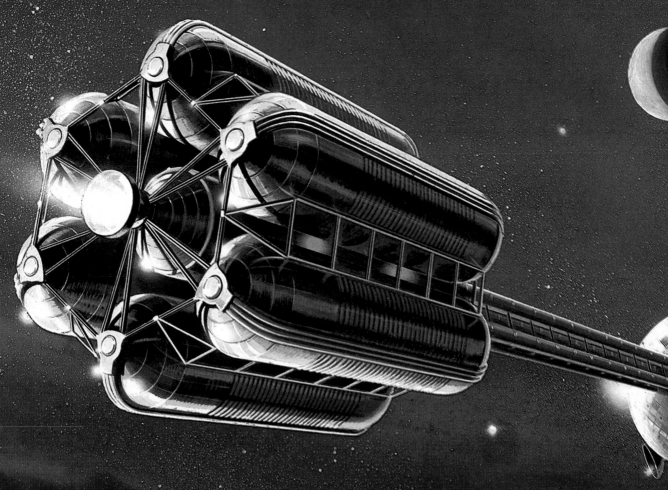

In 1930, astronomers discovered yet another planet when they took photographs of the same stars on different nights. The photographs showed a tiny speck moving across the fixed stars far out in space (shown by the red arrows). This was Pluto. We still know very little about it, but it must be a dark and frozen world.

One day, nuclear-powered spacecraft like the one in the picture may travel further into space and discover even more distant planets!

The Sun

Our Sun is a huge ball of burning gas, over a hundred times wider than the Earth. It is 150 million kilometres away from us, which is still very close compared to the other stars in the Universe. Its rays of light take only eight minutes to reach us, while light from the next star, Alpha Centauri, takes four years!

Without the heat and light we get from the Sun, no life could exist on Earth. The hottest part of the Sun is the centre, which is an unimaginable 15 million degrees centigrade.

On the Sun's surface, storms and dark patches of cooler gas, called sunspots, are often seen. Scientists think that sunspots could affect our weather on Earth. And the storms produce huge loops of flame, called flares, which can cause interference on our radio and television sets.

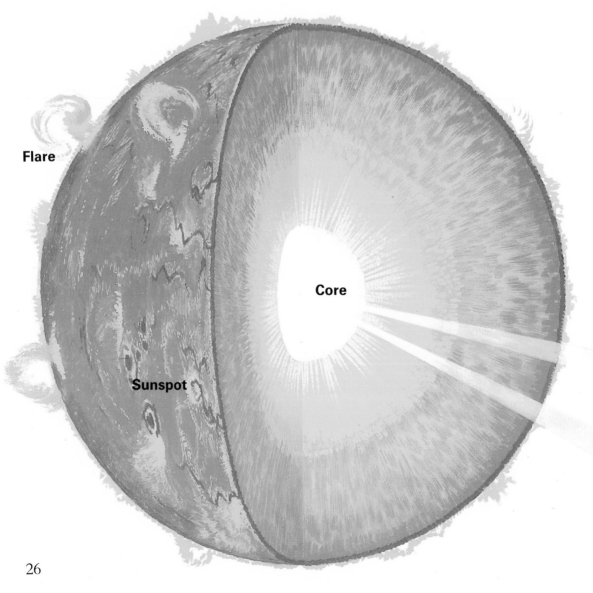

Flare

Sunspot

Core

Cloud of gas and dust

Star shrinks

Birth and Death of a Star

Although the Sun is so important to us, it is quite an ordinary star compared with others in the Universe. The giant star Betelgeuse, for example, is hundreds of times bigger than the Sun.

Astronomers think that all stars are born from giant clouds of gas and dust, called nebulae. Nebulae look like a hazy glowing patch in the night sky, and sometimes you can see them without a telescope.

One nebula can give birth to a whole cluster of stars. As it spins around in space, parts of the cloud become drawn together to form a huge blob of gas. Slowly, the blob begins to shrink until the pressure at

Above: This famous nebula can be seen in the group of stars called Orion. It is lit up by the stars that have formed within it.

Star expands

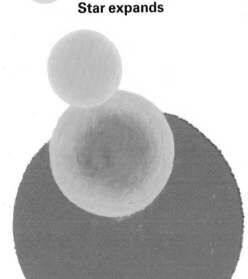

The core of the Sun is incredibly hot. It produces energy which pours out into space, and which gives warmth and light to the Earth.

White dwarf o

its centre creates heat, and it begins to glow. And so a new star is born – to shine in the night sky for millions of years.

Towards the end of its life, a star begins to use up all its energy. It becomes bigger again, and its surface cools from white to red heat. Astronomers call this a red giant.

At last, the thin outer layers of gas drift off into space, rather like a huge smoke ring. This is called a planetary nebula. At the centre of the planetary nebula is the remains of the star – a tiny 'white dwarf'. The white dwarf star is at least 10,000 times smaller than the red giant from which it formed, but it is very heavy. Just one spoonful would weigh 10 tonnes. Over millions of years, it will finally cool and fade away altogether.

One day this will happen to our own Sun. It will swell into a red giant, swallowing Mercury, Venus and possibly the Earth. As the Sun gets nearer and nearer, the ice caps will melt and eventually all the seas will dry up. The Earth will be left as a parched and lifeless cinder.

But at the moment, the Sun is only middle-aged. It is not expected to turn into a red giant for another 5000 million years!

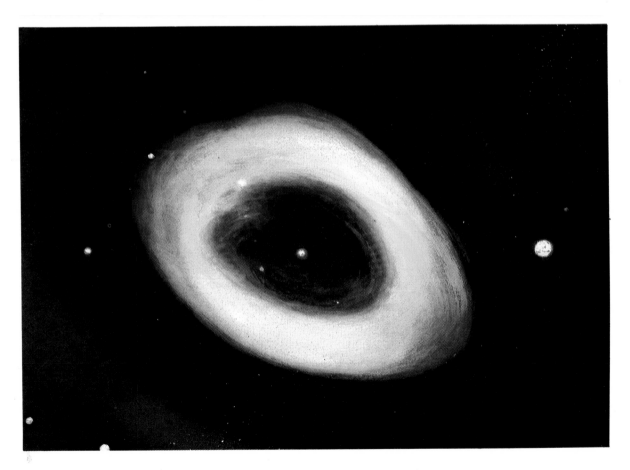

Supernovae

Some stars live longer than others. The bigger and brighter they are, the sooner they burn themselves out. The heaviest stars of all die very dramatically. They become red giants, then shatter into pieces in a spectacular explosion called a supernova. The star appears billions of times brighter as it showers its outer layers into space. In 1054, Chinese astronomers saw a star explode like this. Its shattered remains can still be seen as the beautiful Crab Nebula (right).

Sometimes, the star's core is left behind. This is called a neutron star, and it is so small and faint that it is almost invisible. Astronomers can spot neutron stars by the pulse of radio waves they give out as they spin, rather like the beam from a lighthouse.

Black Holes

Sometimes, the core left after a supernova explosion is unusually heavy. If it is more than three times heavier than our Sun, something very extraordinary happens. Because it is so heavy, the gravity of the core is so strong that it pulls itself inwards. The core shrinks slowly out of sight, and becomes a bottomless pit in the Universe – a black hole. Nothing escapes the pull of the black hole's gravity – even the star's own light disappears, making it completely invisible. And anything unfortunate enough to pass close to the black hole will vanish into its depths forever!

Special Stars

Some stars give off a steady light, but others appear to flicker. These are known as variable stars. Red giants are some of the most common of these.

Some other stars flare up for a short time only. They suddenly become much brighter than they were before, making it possible for astronomers to see them for the first time. These stars are called 'novae',

from the Latin word meaning 'new'. Unlike supernovae, the stars do not blow up altogether, and may flare up many times. But they never become as bright as a supernova.

Unlike the Sun, most stars are not alone in space, but exist in pairs or groups. These are called 'double' or 'multiple' stars.

Double stars can be very different from each other, like the ones in the picture. The big star is the red giant Zeta Aurigae, which is orbited by a small blue star.

The Milky Way

The Sun is just one of the huge cluster of stars that make up our galaxy. If we could see the galaxy from far off in space, it would look like a giant Catherine wheel – as shown above. The white arrow shows the position of our Sun.

On a dark night, we can see the stars at the furthest ends of the galaxy. But because they are so far away, all we see is a distant band of white light. It is this that gives our galaxy its name – the Milky Way.

We used to think that the Milky Way was the whole of the Universe, but in the 1920s an American astronomer called Edwin Hubble noticed a faint glimmer far out in space. Through a telescope he discovered that these were the stars of another galaxy. Astronomers call this the Andromeda galaxy, and it is

Only about half of the galaxies in the Universe are spiral-shaped like the Milky Way.

About a quarter of the known galaxies are barred spirals (top), which have a bar of stars across the centre. Most of the remaining galaxies have an oval shape (above). These are called lenticular galaxies.

an incredible two million 'light years' away. A light year is the distance that a beam of light travels in a year – and light travels at 300,000 kilometres per second. This means that we are now seeing the light that left Andromeda two million years ago – so the galaxy may not even be there any more!

How It All Began

Edwin Hubble discovered many more galaxies in space. And as he looked deeper into the Universe, he made the astounding discovery that the galaxies were all moving apart from one another at high speed. This means that the Universe is getting bigger all the time.

No one really knows how the Universe began. Astronomers think that at one time all the matter in the Universe – the rocks, dust and gas – was packed together tightly in one spot. Then thousands of millions of years ago, there was a huge explosion called the Big Bang. All the matter flew far out into space, where it formed the galaxies.

This still leaves many questions unanswered. We do not know where the matter came from in the first place. And what caused the huge explosion is still a mystery.

Big Bang

The Arizona Meteorite Crater

Comets and Meteors

On any clear night, you can see shooting stars streak across the sky. These are not really stars at all, but meteors – pieces of dust often only the size of a grain of sand which burn up as they hit the Earth's atmosphere. Their blaze of glory lasts for less than a second.

Sometimes, lumps of rock and metal called meteorites crash into the Earth from space. A meteorite travelling fast enough can gouge out an enormous crater like the one in the Arizona desert in America, shown above. It is thought that this crater was made 20,000 years ago.

Meteorites are pieces that have broken off an asteroid or a comet. Asteroids are like small, lumpy planets. They are made up from the rubble that remained in space when the solar system was formed.

Comets are loose pieces of rock and dust, packed together with frozen gas. They travel through space on long, looping orbits. For most of its life, a comet wanders in the dark outer regions of the solar system where we cannot see it. But from time to time, its orbit brings it nearer to the Sun. As it warms up and glows, gas and dust stream away from its 'head' in a spectacular flowing 'tail'.

The most famous is Halley's Comet, which returns every 76 years. It will next appear in 1986. It was once thought that Halley's Comet was the star seen by the Three Wise Men in the Bible story.

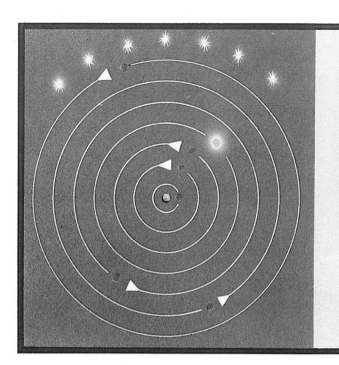

Ancient astronomers discovered five 'wandering stars', or planets. They named them after their gods – Mercury, Venus, Mars, Jupiter and Saturn. Their maps put the Earth at the centre of the Universe, with the Sun and the planets circling around it.

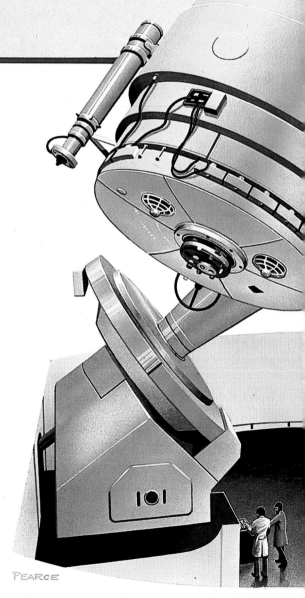

Exploring Space

Astronomers have studied the sky through telescopes for hundreds of years. By using lenses and mirrors, a telescope can collect more light than the human eye. This makes distant planets and stars appear much closer.

By studying the colours in the light around a planet, scientists can find out what the atmosphere is made up of. Telescopes can also collect heat, so they can take a planet's temperature. Scientists can even work out how much a planet weighs, by watching the effect of its gravity on the path of other nearby planets and moons.

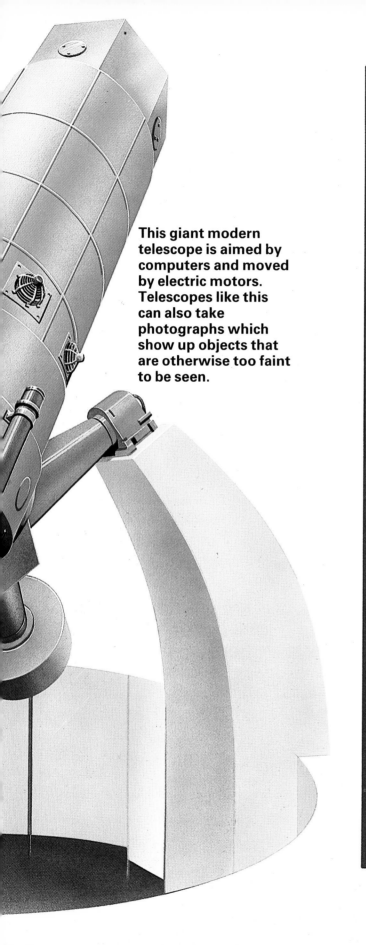

This giant modern telescope is aimed by computers and moved by electric motors. Telescopes like this can also take photographs which show up objects that are otherwise too faint to be seen.

Astronomers also use radio telescopes to study space. These 'see' faraway planets rather like radar sets 'see' distant aircraft.

Radio telescopes work by sending signals out into space. When a signal hits a planet, it bounces back to Earth as an echo. Astronomers can work out how far away a planet is by the time it takes for the echo to bounce back to Earth.

Radio telescopes can also help astronomers to map a planet's surface. An echo from a high mountain bounces back before one hitting flat ground.

Leaving the Earth

Since the invention of the rocket, we can take a much closer look at the Universe. Space probes send back close-up photographs of distant planets, and laboratories orbit the Earth.

The *Saturn 5* rocket in the picture was used to send the Apollo spacecraft to the Moon. You can see how huge it was compared to the cars and helicopters. The small spacecraft which carried the astronauts and the Moon landing vehicle was attached to the top of the rocket.

Saturn 5 was really three rockets joined together. Each one had a powerful engine which fell to Earth as soon as its fuel had burned out.

Saturn 5

Rocket hangar

The first rocket was the most powerful, and was used for the launch. As mission control counted down the final seconds to blast-off, a great flame lit up the rocket and it rose slowly into the air. When all the fuel was used up, the first stage fell away, making the rest of the rocket much lighter.

The second stage then took over, and finally the third rocket carried the spacecraft out beyond the gravity of the Earth. The final part of the Moon journey was made using the power of the spacecraft's own engines.

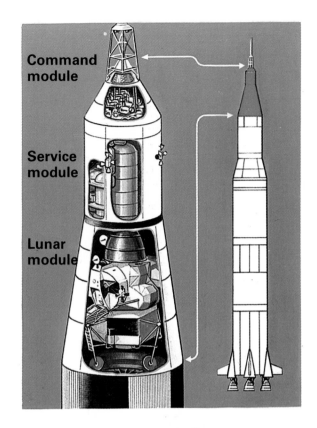

Command module

Service module

Lunar module

Transporter

Blast-off

Saturn 5

People in Space

Vostok 1

Gemini 4

The *Apollo* Moon landing followed many years of preparation by both the USA and the USSR.

The first man to travel in space was a Soviet cosmonaut called Yuri Gagarin. 'Cosmonaut' is the Russian word for 'astronaut', or space traveller. In 1961, Gagarin orbited the Earth once in his spacecraft *Vostok 1*.

In 1965, Alexei Leonov of the USSR crawled through a hatch in his spacecraft and made the first space 'walk'. A few weeks later, the American astronaut Edward White made a similar walk from *Gemini 4*.

To send people into space, a spacecraft must be carefully designed with enough air, electricity and food supplies to last the journey. The temperature must be controlled, and a heat shield is needed to protect the craft from burning up as it speeds back through the Earth's atmosphere on its return journey.

The *Apollo 11* spacecraft was made up of three separate parts, called 'modules'. The three astronauts travelled in the command module, which was connected to a service module. Under this was the lunar module, which took Neil Armstrong and Edwin Aldrin down to the Moon's surface.

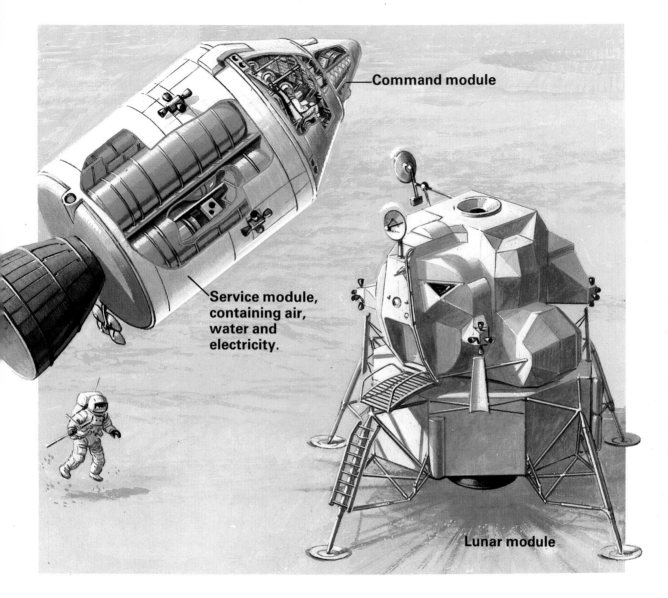

Command module

Service module, containing air, water and electricity.

Lunar module

The lunar module was called the *Eagle*, and it was made up of two halves. The bottom half had landing legs and contained the engine which took the module to the Moon's surface. It also acted as a launching pad when the top half blasted-off to rejoin the orbiting command module piloted by Michael Collins.

Because the Moon's gravity is much weaker than the Earth's, much less speed was needed to boost the *Eagle* off the Moon than was needed to launch *Apollo 11* from Earth.

To make the journey home, *Apollo 11* fired its main engine. When it neared Earth, the landing parachutes opened and the spacecraft made a gentle splash-down into the sea.

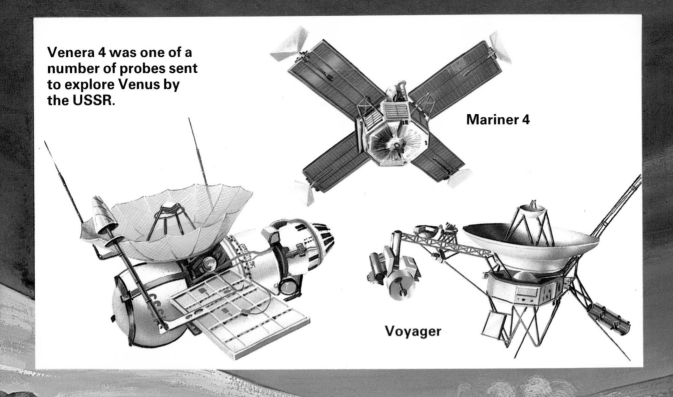

Venera 4 was one of a number of probes sent to explore Venus by the USSR.

Mariner 4

Voyager

Probes to the Planets

We are not yet ready to send people to visit the other planets of our solar system. But until we are, we can launch computer-controlled space probes ahead to explore the outer reaches of space.

The first probes to reach another planet were the *Mariner* series. These flew past Mars, Venus and Mercury, and prepared the way for the successful landing of the *Viking* spacecraft on the Martian surface. *Viking* used mechanical 'arms' to scoop up soil. It then tested it and radioed the results back to Earth.

Even far-off Jupiter and Saturn have been explored by probes. These planets were first photographed by the *Pioneer* series. Since then, two more advanced *Voyager* probes have sent back spectacular colour pictures of the swirling clouds above Jupiter. The *Voyager* probes then travelled on to Saturn, and should reach Uranus in 1986 and Neptune in 1989. As they travel through space, they play recordings of Earth sounds such as animal cries – just in case anyone is out there listening!

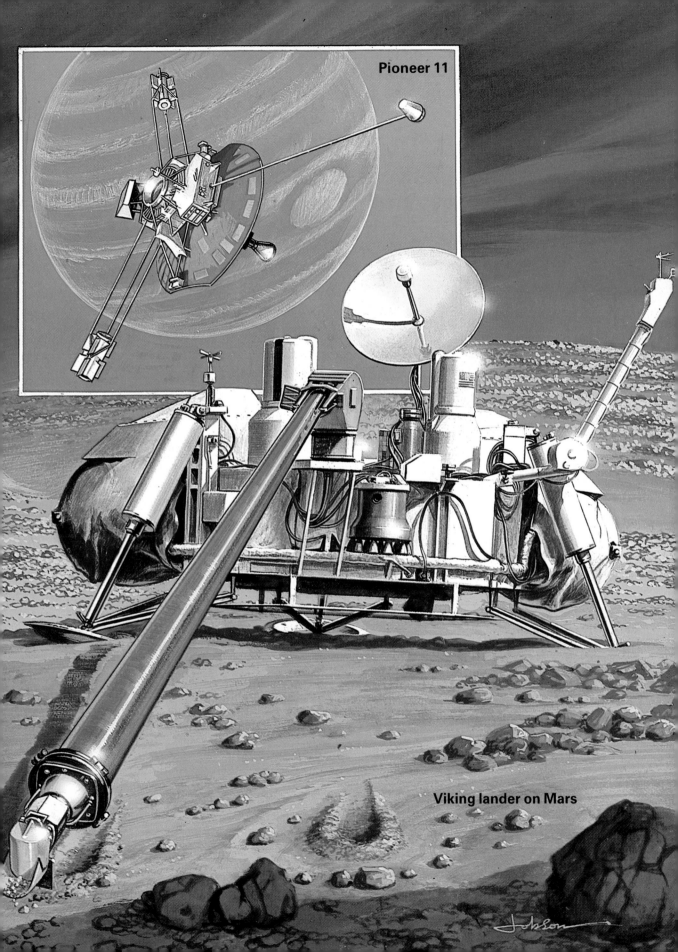

Pioneer 11

Viking lander on Mars

Space Stations

While the USA was busy getting a man on the Moon, the Soviet Union was more interested in setting up a large scientific station in space. In 1971, *Salyut 1* became the first space station to orbit the Earth.

In 1973, the US space team put *Skylab* into orbit. Twice as big as *Salyut*, *Skylab* had many serious problems to begin with. During the launch, a heat shield was torn off, and so was one of the solar panels. These turned the Sun's rays into electricity, and were needed to power the space station. However, *Skylab's* first crew carried out successful repairs, and put up a sunshade in place of the heat shield.

Space stations are larger than ordinary spacecraft, and a crew of astronauts can live and work there for several months at a time.

The stars and planets can be seen more clearly from the space station than from Earth, because in space there is no atmosphere to stop light getting through. The astronauts can also send back valuable information about the Earth itself.

As well as observing the planets, the astronauts were able to discover whether people could

survive in space for long periods of time. This is very important if people are ever going to travel to distant planets.

Because there is no gravity in empty space, objects become weightless and float around. Bodies become weaker, and astronauts must take a lot of exercise to keep fit. But all the astronauts who lived in *Salyut* and *Skylab* managed to stay healthy, and doctors now think that people could live comfortably in space for about a year – long enough to reach Mars.

Space stations of the future may be used to build enormous spacecraft out in space, far away from the pull of the Earth's gravity.

Space shuttle

A New Era in Space

Until the invention of the space shuttle, all rockets and spacecraft could only be used once. After that, they had to be scrapped.

The space shuttle is launched by two rockets, which parachute back to Earth and can be used again. When the shuttle has finished its journey in space it glides back to Earth just like an aircraft. After being carefully checked over, it can then be used again.

Space shuttles will now make it possible to build cheaper and bigger space stations. They can also put man-made satellites into orbit around the Earth. Satellites are used for many purposes, from studying the weather to carrying TV and telephone signals all over the world.

Space shuttles would also play an important part in building huge space colonies, like the one in the picture. These would be big enough for thousands of people to live in permanently, and would be made to look as much like the Earth as possible. Huge mirrors could reflect sunlight through windows, so the colony would be able to grow its own food and make electricity.

The main problem would be the weightlessness of space. Without gravity, the people of the colonies

would float about helplessly. Liquids would not pour from bottles, and washing and eating would cause water and food to fly about everywhere! However, colonies could be built in the shape of a giant wheel, which could spin around to create an artificial gravity.

Space colonies could be very important if the Earth became overcrowded. We are also using up our mineral supplies on Earth, and in the future, colonies may be set up to mine the Moon and other planets.

Starships will have to reach incredible speeds if we are ever to explore other solar systems. The nearest star, Alpha Centauri, is light years away. Maybe one day, huge nuclear-powered spacecraft will set out to visit the distant stars. But the people who arrive there will be many generations younger that the travellers who began the voyage.

Strange Visitors

For many years, scientists have wondered whether there is life somewhere out in space. Although we have found no life on the other planets in our solar system, there are thousands of millions of stars in our galaxy alone. Any one of these stars could have a solar system very like our own, with life forms at least as intelligent as those on Earth.

Many people have reported seeing strange objects in the sky. Some are just glowing balls of light, while others look like the 'flying saucer' shown in the picture. These are known as Unidentified Flying Objects, or UFOs. Many have turned out to be objects such as aeroplanes or meteors. Satellites in the night sky can also be mistaken for UFOs, and there have even been some deliberate fakes. But many people believe that UFOs are spaceships from distant parts of the Universe, cautiously watching the Earth.

Seeing a UFO nearby is called a 'close encounter'. A close encounter of the first kind is a sighting of a UFO close in the sky. No contact is made, and the UFO does not land.

In a close encounter of the second kind, people find traces of the UFO as well as seeing it. For example, a UFO might jam a radio signal, or cause a car engine to fail. If it lands, it may leave marks on the ground.

The most extraordinary sightings are close encounters of the third kind, when living creatures are seen in or near the UFO. One such sighting took place in 1964 in New Mexico, USA, when a policeman noticed a silver oval-shaped object parked off the road. Standing nearby were two human-like people, about the size of ten-year-old children. As he approached, the creatures entered their craft and it took off with a deafening roar. Where the craft had been, there were strange scorch marks on the ground.

Are we visited by 'ufonauts' from other parts of the galaxy? If so, they must come from a more highly developed world than our own. Our spacecraft could not reach even the nearest stars. For the time being, UFOs remain just one of the many mysteries of the Universe.

Index

*Page references refer
to main entries only*